Submerged Visions: Capturing the Wonders of Underwater Photography

Welcome to the mesmerizing world beneath the waves, where beauty, mystery, and wonder converge. "Submerged Visions: Capturing the Wonders of Underwater Photography" invites you to embark on a captivating journey into the depths, exploring the extraordinary realm of underwater photography. In this book, we delve into the art and technique of capturing stunning images beneath the water's surface, revealing the hidden treasures and enchanting creatures that inhabit the underwater world.

Through the lens of talented photographers and the insights of experienced divers, this book illuminates the challenges and rewards of underwater photography. From vibrant coral reefs to graceful marine life, each page showcases the breathtaking moments frozen in time, offering a glimpse into a realm that is both serene and exhilarating.

As you turn the pages, you will discover the secrets behind capturing those awe-inspiring shots, from the technical aspects of underwater equipment and lighting to the artistic composition that brings the underwater landscapes to life. Dive deep into the intricacies of capturing motion, color, and texture in this dynamic environment, and gain a deeper appreciation for the artistry and skill required to convey the essence of underwater beauty through photography.

"Submerged Visions" also celebrates the vital role of conservation and preservation in safeguarding these fragile ecosystems. It highlights the importance of ethical practices and responsible interactions with marine life, inspiring readers to become advocates for the preservation of our oceans.

Whether you are an aspiring underwater photographer or simply a lover of the natural world, this book will transport you to a realm of awe-inspiring beauty, where the visual spectacle of underwater photography unfolds before your eyes. Join us on this exploration of "Submerged Visions: Capturing the Wonders of Underwater Photography" and immerse yourself in the captivating allure of the underwater realm.

I. Introduction

- The allure of underwater photography
- Invitation to explore the hidden world beneath the waves

II. The Art of Underwater Photography

- Understanding the unique challenges and techniques
- Capturing the beauty and serenity of underwater landscapes
- Conveying emotions through underwater photography

III. Marine Life and Biodiversity

- Showcasing the stunning diversity of marine species

- Exploring the delicate balance of marine ecosystems
- Conservation and raising awareness through photography

IV. Underwater Photography Equipment and Gear

- Essential equipment for capturing underwater shots
- Camera settings and techniques for optimal results
- Tips for protecting gear and ensuring safety underwater

V. Exploring Underwater Wonders

- Coral reefs and their vibrant ecosystems
- Marine wildlife encounters and capturing their natural behavior
- Underwater caves, shipwrecks, and other intriguing environments

VI. Underwater Photography as a Medium of Storytelling

- Conveying narratives through underwater images
- Environmental issues and the power of visual storytelling
- Inspiring conservation efforts through photography

VII. Underwater Photography Expeditions and Adventures

- Planning and preparing for underwater photography trips
- Destination highlights and must-visit underwater photography spots

VIII. Post-Processing and Sharing Underwater Images

- Editing techniques for enhancing underwater photographs
- Platforms for showcasing and sharing underwater photography

- Engaging with the underwater photography community

IX. The Future of Underwater Photography

- Technological advancements and their impact on the field
- Trends and emerging styles in underwater photography
- The role of underwater photography in conservation and education

X. Conclusion

- Reflection on the beauty and importance of underwater photography
- Call to action for readers to explore and appreciate the underwater world
- Final thoughts on the captivating journey of Submerged Visions

The allure of underwater photography

Underwater photography has a unique allure that captivates both photographers and viewers alike. It offers a mesmerizing and otherworldly perspective, showcasing the beauty and mysteries of the underwater realm. Here are some aspects that contribute to the allure of underwater photography:

1. Exploration and Discovery: Underwater photography allows us to explore a world that is largely inaccessible to us. It takes us beneath the surface of the water, unveiling a vast and diverse ecosystem filled with vibrant marine life, coral reefs, underwater caves, and shipwrecks. It gives us a sense of adventure and discovery as we encounter new and fascinating subjects.

2. Visual Appeal: The underwater world is a visual feast for the eyes. The play of light, colors, and textures underwater creates stunning and ethereal imagery. The transparency of the water, the interplay of sunlight, and the vibrant hues of marine life combine to create visually striking compositions that evoke a sense of awe and wonder.

3. Unique Subjects: Underwater photography offers a wide range of unique subjects that are not commonly seen on land. From colorful coral reefs teeming with fish and other marine creatures to graceful sea turtles, majestic sharks, and delicate seahorses, the underwater world is home to a diverse array of fascinating subjects that make for compelling photographs.

4. Sense of Serenity and Tranquility: Being immersed in the underwater environment provides a sense

of serenity and tranquility. The silence, the weightlessness, and the feeling of being in harmony with nature create a peaceful and calming experience. Underwater photography allows us to capture and convey this sense of tranquility, creating images that evoke a feeling of serenity and escape.

5. Conservation and Awareness: Underwater photography also plays a crucial role in raising awareness about the fragile nature of underwater ecosystems and the need for their conservation. By capturing and sharing captivating images of the underwater world, photographers can inspire viewers to appreciate and protect these delicate environments, promoting conservation efforts and sustainable practices.

6. Technical Challenge: Underwater photography presents unique technical challenges. Dealing with low light, water currents, limited visibility, and the need for specialized equipment requires skill, knowledge, and adaptability. Overcoming these challenges and successfully capturing stunning images underwater adds an element of excitement and accomplishment for photographers.

7. Storytelling and Education: Underwater photography has the power to tell stories and educate viewers about the importance of marine life and ecosystems. Through captivating images, photographers can convey the beauty, fragility, and interconnectedness of the underwater world, inspiring viewers to appreciate and protect these environments.

8. Personal Connection with Nature: Underwater photography provides an opportunity to connect with nature on a deeper level. The close proximity to marine life and the immersive experience underwater foster a sense of connection and empathy with the natural world. This connection can be profoundly rewarding and can create a lasting impact on photographers and

viewers alike.

Whether you are an aspiring photographer or an admirer of the beauty beneath the waves, underwater photography offers a fascinating and alluring world to explore. It combines adventure, artistic expression, and conservation efforts, inviting us to appreciate the wonders of the underwater realm and to protect it for future generations.

Invitation to explore the hidden world beneath the waves

Beneath the waves lies a hidden world of awe-inspiring beauty and fascinating creatures, waiting to be discovered and explored. It's an invitation to dive into the depths and immerse yourself in the wonders of the underwater realm.

Take a plunge into the crystal-clear waters and witness the vibrant colors of coral reefs, swaying in harmony with the currents. Marvel at the graceful movements of sea turtles as they glide through the water, or the curious antics of playful dolphins and seals. Swim alongside majestic sharks, their sleek forms commanding respect and awe.

Discover the intricate patterns and textures of marine life, from the delicate fronds of sea anemones to the intricate shells of seashells. Observe the symbiotic relationships between different species, as fish dart in and out of coral formations, seeking shelter and sustenance.

Capture these extraordinary moments through the lens of underwater photography, freezing time and preserving the magic of the underwater world. Share your experiences and stories, allowing others to glimpse the wonders that lie beneath the surface.

But exploring the underwater world goes beyond the visual spectacle. It's an opportunity to connect with nature on a profound level, to feel the weightlessness and serenity as you dive deeper into the depths. It's a reminder of the fragility and interconnectedness of our planet, and the importance of preserving these delicate ecosystems.

So, grab your snorkel or scuba gear, and embark on an adventure of a lifetime. Whether you're an experienced diver or a curious beginner, the underwater world has something to offer everyone. Explore reefs, wrecks, and underwater caves. Dive into different locations around the world, each with its own unique marine life and underwater landscapes.

Immerse yourself in the hidden world beneath the waves, and let it inspire you, captivate you, and remind you of the beauty and resilience of our oceans. Take the plunge, and let the wonders of the underwater world leave an indelible mark on your soul.

Understanding the unique challenges and techniques

Underwater photography presents its own set of challenges and requires specialized techniques to capture stunning images in the aquatic environment. Here are some key considerations and techniques to help you navigate the world of underwater photography:

1. Equipment: Invest in quality underwater photography equipment, including a waterproof camera or a housing for your existing camera. Choose a camera with good low-light performance, fast autofocus, and a wide-angle lens for capturing expansive underwater scenes.

2. Lighting: Underwater photography often suffers from low light conditions and color distortion. To counteract this, use artificial lighting sources such as strobes or underwater flashes. These can help illuminate your subject and restore natural colors.

3. Composition: Composition plays a crucial role in underwater photography. Consider the position and angle of your subject, the surrounding marine life, and the overall scene. Aim to create visually interesting compositions that convey a sense of depth and perspective.

4. Buoyancy and stability: Achieving buoyancy control and maintaining stability underwater is essential for capturing sharp images. Practice good diving skills to minimize disturbances to the marine environment and position yourself steadily for capturing the desired

shots.

5. Depth and water clarity: Different depths and water conditions can affect the quality and visibility of your images. Experiment with different depths to find the optimal lighting conditions and clarity for capturing your subjects.

6. Patience and observation: Underwater photography requires patience and keen observation. Take your time to study the behavior of marine life and wait for the right moments to capture captivating shots. Be aware of your surroundings and anticipate the movements of your subjects.

7. Post-processing: Post-processing is often necessary to enhance your underwater images. Adjustments to color balance, contrast, and sharpness can help restore the natural beauty of the underwater scene. Experiment with editing techniques to bring out the best in your photos.

8. Safety and conservation: Prioritize safety and environmental conservation when engaging in underwater photography. Respect marine life and their habitats, adhere to dive guidelines, and avoid touching or disturbing the underwater ecosystem. Be mindful of your own limitations and ensure you are adequately trained and equipped for underwater photography.

By understanding and applying these techniques, you can overcome the unique challenges of underwater photography and capture stunning images that showcase the enchanting beauty of the underwater world. Embrace the adventure, hone your skills, and let your underwater photography transport viewers to a captivating realm they may have never experienced before.

Capturing the beauty and serenity of underwater landscapes

Underwater landscapes possess a unique and captivating beauty that can be truly mesmerizing. Here are some tips for capturing the serenity and beauty of underwater landscapes through photography:

1. Seek clear water: Look for locations with clear water and good visibility to capture the intricate details and vibrant colors of the underwater landscape. Visibility can vary depending on factors such as water currents, tides, and weather conditions, so research and choose the best time and location for your shoot.

2. Explore different depths: Underwater landscapes can vary greatly depending on the depth you explore. Experiment with shooting at different depths to capture the unique features and transitions of the underwater terrain. Deeper areas may reveal more dramatic seascapes, while shallower areas can showcase vibrant coral reefs or underwater rock formations.

3. Utilize wide-angle lenses: Wide-angle lenses are ideal for capturing expansive underwater landscapes. They allow you to include more of the scene in your frame and create a sense of depth and scale. Wide-angle lenses also help capture the play of light and shadow underwater, adding to the overall aesthetic appeal of the image.

4. Incorporate natural light: Natural light filtering through the water can create stunning effects in underwater landscapes. Pay attention to the angle and intensity

of the sunlight to capture the desired mood and atmosphere. Experiment with shooting towards the surface to capture beautiful sun rays penetrating the water or shooting against the light to create silhouettes.

5. Capture movement and flow: Underwater landscapes are often characterized by the fluid motion of water and marine life. Look for opportunities to capture the movement and flow, whether it's the gentle sway of seaweed, the graceful glide of fish, or the swirling patterns created by currents. Incorporating movement adds dynamism and visual interest to your images.

6. Focus on details: While capturing the grandeur of underwater landscapes, don't forget to focus on the intricate details that make them unique. Explore the textures, patterns, and colors of coral formations, rocks, and marine life up close. Macro lenses or close-up filters can help you capture the minute details and reveal the hidden beauty of the underwater world.

7. Experiment with different angles and perspectives: Change your shooting angles and perspectives to add variety and visual interest to your underwater landscape photographs. Shoot from different positions —above, below, or at eye level—to capture different viewpoints and unique compositions. Play with reflections and use the water's surface as a creative element in your images.

8. Post-processing enhancements: Post-processing can help enhance the beauty and impact of your underwater landscape images. Adjustments to color balance, contrast, and saturation can bring out the vibrant colors and details captured underwater. Use editing software to fine-tune your images while maintaining a natural and realistic look.

Remember to always prioritize safety and respect for the underwater environment when photographing underwater landscapes. Follow proper diving protocols, be aware of your surroundings, and avoid damaging or disturbing marine life and their habitats. With patience, practice, and a keen eye for detail, you can capture the beauty and serenity of underwater landscapes and share the wonders of the underwater world with others.

Conveying emotions through underwater photography

Underwater photography offers a unique platform to convey emotions and capture the awe-inspiring beauty of the underwater world. Here are some techniques to help you convey emotions through your underwater photographs:

1. Use lighting creatively: Lighting plays a crucial role in setting the mood and evoking emotions in your underwater images. Experiment with different lighting techniques to create dramatic effects. Play with shadows, silhouettes, and the interplay of light and water to convey a sense of mystery, tranquility, or excitement.

2. Focus on expressions: If you're photographing human subjects underwater, pay attention to their expressions and body language. Emotions can be conveyed through facial expressions, gestures, and the way the subject interacts with the underwater environment. Capture genuine moments of joy, wonder, or contemplation to evoke emotions in your viewers.

3. Explore color psychology: Colors have a strong impact on our emotions. Underwater photography presents a unique color palette, with vibrant blues, greens, and an array of other hues. Different colors can evoke different emotions, such as calmness with shades of blue, vitality with vibrant yellows and oranges, or serenity with soft pastels. Use color intentionally to create the desired emotional impact in your images.

4. Capture dynamic movements: Emotions can be expressed through movement in underwater photography. Whether it's the graceful swim of marine life, the playfulness of dolphins, or the powerful strokes of a diver, capturing dynamic movements can convey energy, excitement, or a sense of freedom. Freeze the action with fast shutter speeds or experiment with slower shutter speeds to create motion blur and convey a sense of fluidity.

5. Pay attention to composition: Composition plays a significant role in conveying emotions in any form of photography. Use compositional techniques such as leading lines, symmetry, and the rule of thirds to guide the viewer's eye and evoke specific emotions. Experiment with different perspectives and framing to create a sense of intimacy or vastness, depending on the emotion you want to convey.

6. Include storytelling elements: Emotions are often evoked through storytelling. Incorporate elements in your underwater photographs that tell a story or evoke a narrative. This can be the interaction between marine life, the presence of human subjects, or the inclusion of symbolic objects or underwater landscapes that have cultural or personal significance.

7. Experiment with post-processing: Post-processing can enhance the emotional impact of your underwater images. Adjusting contrast, saturation, and tone can bring out the desired mood and atmosphere. Experiment with different styles and effects to evoke specific emotions, whether it's creating a dreamy and ethereal look or a bold and dramatic atmosphere.

Remember that conveying emotions in underwater photography requires a deep connection with your subject and a keen observation of the underwater environment. Be patient, be present, and allow yourself to feel and capture the emotions that arise during your underwater adventures. By harnessing the power of composition, lighting, color, and storytelling, you can create impactful underwater images that resonate with viewers and evoke a wide range of emotions.

Showcasing the stunning diversity of marine species

The world beneath the waves is teeming with an incredible diversity of marine species, each with its own unique beauty and charm. Here are some ways to showcase the stunning diversity of marine species in your underwater photography:

1. Macro photography: Use a macro lens or macro mode to capture the intricate details of small marine creatures such as nudibranchs, seahorses, or tiny fish. Focus on the fascinating textures, patterns, and colors that make these creatures so captivating.

2. Wide-angle shots: Capture the vastness and grandeur of the underwater world by using a wide-angle lens. This allows you to include expansive seascapes, coral reefs, and schools of fish in a single frame. Wide-angle shots provide a sense of scale and emphasize the diversity of marine life in their natural habitats.

3. Close-up portraits: Zoom in on the faces and unique features of larger marine animals like sharks, dolphins, or sea turtles. Capture their expressions and personalities to showcase the individuality and beauty of these majestic creatures.

4. Behavior and interaction: Capture the dynamic interactions and behaviors of marine species to highlight their natural behaviors and relationships. Whether it's a fish hunting, a sea turtle gliding through the water, or a coral reef bustling with activity, these shots can tell compelling stories about the lives of

marine animals.

5. Colorful reefs and habitats: Showcase the vibrant and colorful underwater ecosystems, including coral reefs and kelp forests. These habitats are home to a myriad of marine species and provide a stunning backdrop for your photographs. Capture the intricate textures, patterns, and variety of life within these environments.

6. Unusual and rare species: Seek out lesser-known or rare marine species to showcase their uniqueness and capture the attention of viewers. This could be a rare species of fish, an elusive octopus, or a deep-sea creature that few have seen before. These photographs can spark curiosity and raise awareness about the incredible biodiversity in our oceans.

7. Silhouettes and creative lighting: Experiment with lighting techniques to create artistic and visually striking images. Silhouettes against the sun or creative use of natural or artificial lighting can add drama and intrigue to your photos, highlighting the form and contours of marine species in a unique way.

Remember, when photographing marine species, it's important to prioritize their well-being and the conservation of their habitats. Respect the marine environment, maintain a safe distance, and avoid disturbing or stressing the animals. By capturing and sharing the stunning diversity of marine species through your photography, you can inspire others to appreciate and protect the precious ecosystems that they call home.

Exploring the delicate balance
of marine ecosystems

Marine ecosystems are incredibly diverse and interconnected, forming a delicate balance that supports the health and survival of countless species. Exploring this balance is not only fascinating but also crucial for understanding the importance of marine conservation. Here are some aspects to consider when exploring the delicate balance of marine ecosystems:

1. Biodiversity: Marine ecosystems are home to an astounding array of species, from microscopic plankton to massive whales. Each species plays a role in the ecosystem, whether as a predator, prey, or contributor to nutrient cycling. Understanding the interdependencies and relationships between different species is essential for appreciating the delicate balance of marine ecosystems.

2. Trophic levels: Marine food webs illustrate the transfer of energy and nutrients between different organisms. Exploring the trophic levels within a marine ecosystem reveals the intricate connections and dependencies among species. From primary producers like phytoplankton to apex predators like sharks, every organism has a specific role in maintaining the balance of energy flow and resource utilization.

3. Habitat diversity: Marine ecosystems encompass a range of habitats, including coral reefs, seagrass meadows, mangrove forests, and deep-sea environments. Each habitat supports a unique assemblage of species and

contributes to overall ecosystem health. Exploring the characteristics and functions of different habitats provides insight into the diverse roles they play in the larger marine ecosystem.

4. Environmental factors: Factors such as water temperature, salinity, pH, and nutrient availability have a profound impact on the health and balance of marine ecosystems. Understanding how these environmental factors influence the distribution and abundance of species is crucial for assessing the resilience of marine ecosystems to ongoing environmental changes.

5. Human impacts: Human activities, such as overfishing, pollution, habitat destruction, and climate change, pose significant threats to the delicate balance of marine ecosystems. Exploring the impacts of these factors on marine life and ecosystem dynamics can help raise awareness about the need for conservation and sustainable practices to protect the fragile balance of these ecosystems.

6. Resilience and adaptation: Despite the challenges they face, marine ecosystems have remarkable resilience and the ability to adapt to changing conditions. Exploring the mechanisms of resilience and adaptation within marine ecosystems can provide insights into how these systems can recover and thrive even in the face of disturbances.

By delving into the delicate balance of marine ecosystems, we gain a deeper appreciation for the interconnectedness of all life in the oceans. It reinforces the importance of conservation efforts to preserve the health and integrity of these ecosystems, ensuring their continued existence for future generations.

Conservation and raising awareness through photography

Underwater photography has the power to raise awareness and inspire action for marine conservation. By capturing captivating images of marine life and ecosystems, photographers can convey the beauty, fragility, and importance of the underwater world. Here are some ways in which underwater photography can contribute to conservation and raise awareness:

1. Visual storytelling: Compelling photographs have the ability to tell stories and evoke emotions. By capturing images of marine life, habitats, and conservation efforts, photographers can create visual narratives that engage viewers and generate empathy for the marine environment.

2. Education and outreach: Underwater photographs can be used in educational materials, presentations, exhibitions, and online platforms to educate the public about the importance of marine conservation. Through the power of visuals, photographers can convey information about marine ecosystems, species diversity, threats, and conservation solutions.

3. Conservation campaigns: Underwater photographs can be used as powerful tools in conservation campaigns. They can be featured in magazines, websites, social media platforms, and other media outlets to draw attention to specific conservation issues, highlight success stories, and promote responsible behavior towards the marine environment.

4. Building connections: Through their photographs, underwater photographers can help people develop a personal connection with the underwater world. By showcasing the beauty and diversity of marine life, they can inspire a sense of wonder and curiosity, motivating individuals to become more engaged in marine conservation efforts.

5. Documenting change: Underwater photographers have the opportunity to document changes in marine ecosystems over time. By capturing images of threatened species, damaged habitats, and the impacts of human activities, photographers can provide visual evidence of the need for conservation action and the urgency of protecting these fragile environments.

6. Collaboration with researchers and organizations: Underwater photographers can collaborate with marine biologists, conservation organizations, and research institutions to document and communicate their work. By capturing images of scientific research, conservation projects, and conservation success stories, photographers contribute to the dissemination of scientific knowledge and conservation achievements.

Through their artistry and storytelling, underwater photographers play a crucial role in raising awareness about the importance of marine conservation. Their work has the potential to inspire individuals, communities, and policymakers to take action and make positive changes for the protection of marine ecosystems and the preservation of our oceans' biodiversity.

Essential equipment for capturing underwater shots

To capture stunning underwater shots, it's important to have the right equipment that is specifically designed for underwater photography. Here are some essential pieces of equipment you'll need:

1. Underwater camera housing: This is a watertight case that protects your camera from water damage. It allows you to operate the camera's controls while submerged. Make sure the housing is compatible with your specific camera model.

2. Camera and lens: Choose a camera that suits your skill level and budget. Look for a camera with manual settings and a good ISO range for low-light conditions. For underwater photography, wide-angle lenses are commonly used to capture expansive underwater landscapes, while macro lenses are ideal for close-up shots of small marine life.

3. Strobes or underwater flashes: Light is quickly absorbed underwater, so strobes or underwater flashes are essential for illuminating your subjects and adding color to your images. Position them strategically to avoid backscatter, which occurs when particles in the water reflect the light back into the camera.

4. Underwater lighting: In addition to strobes, you may also use continuous underwater lighting, such as video lights or dive lights, to enhance the colors and details in your shots. These lights are especially useful for video

recording or shooting in low-light conditions.

5. Lens filters: Underwater lens filters can help correct color distortion caused by water absorption and restore the natural colors in your images. Common filters used in underwater photography include red filters for tropical waters and magenta filters for greenish or blue waters.

6. Buoyancy control devices: Buoyancy control is essential for stability and maneuverability underwater. Consider using buoyancy control devices such as underwater camera trays, arms, and floats to help you achieve steady shots and maintain control of your equipment.

7. Wet lenses and diopters: Wet lenses are additional lenses that can be attached to your camera housing while underwater. They allow for closer focusing distances or wider field of view, enhancing the versatility of your shots. Diopters, which are similar to close-up lenses, can be used for macro photography to capture fine details of small subjects.

8. Underwater camera housing maintenance kit: Proper maintenance of your camera housing is crucial to prevent leaks and ensure its longevity. A maintenance kit typically includes O-rings, lubricants, and cleaning tools to keep your housing in good condition.

Remember to also consider other essentials such as underwater camera straps, dive gloves, and a reliable underwater camera bag or case for transporting your equipment safely.

It's important to note that underwater photography requires specialized skills and knowledge, as well as diving certifications if you plan to dive to greater depths. It's recommended to undergo proper training and practice in controlled environments before venturing into more challenging underwater photography scenarios.

Camera settings and techniques for optimal results

To achieve optimal results in underwater photography, here are some camera settings and techniques to consider:

1. Aperture priority or manual mode: These modes give you control over the aperture setting, which determines the depth of field in your images. For wide-angle shots, use a smaller aperture (higher f-number) like f/8 or f/11 to capture more of the scene in focus. For macro shots, you may want to use a larger aperture (lower f-number) like f/2.8 or f/4 to create a shallow depth of field and isolate your subject.

2. Shutter speed: Use a fast shutter speed to freeze the motion of fast-moving subjects and reduce the risk of blurry images. Depending on the lighting conditions, you may need to adjust your shutter speed accordingly. A starting point can be around 1/125th or 1/250th of a second, but you may need to increase it in brighter conditions or decrease it in darker conditions.

3. ISO: Set your ISO to the lowest possible value to maintain image quality and minimize noise. Start with ISO 100 or 200 and increase it only if necessary due to low light conditions. Be mindful of noise levels when using higher ISO settings.

4. White balance: Underwater lighting can affect the colors in your images, so it's important to set the appropriate white balance. You can use the camera's auto white balance or manually adjust it using custom

white balance settings or underwater color correction filters.

5. Focus modes: For moving subjects, use continuous autofocus (AI Servo, AF-C) to maintain focus as the subject moves. If shooting stationary subjects or macro shots, switch to single autofocus (One Shot, AF-S) and take your time to focus accurately.

6. Composition and framing: Pay attention to composition by using the rule of thirds, leading lines, and interesting angles to create visually appealing images. Experiment with different perspectives to capture unique and compelling underwater scenes.

7. Strobe positioning: Position your strobes or underwater flashes strategically to minimize backscatter and evenly illuminate your subjects. Consider using dual strobes to eliminate shadows and provide more balanced lighting.

8. Continuous shooting mode: Use the continuous shooting mode (burst mode) to capture a series of images in quick succession. This can be useful for capturing fast-moving subjects or ensuring you get the perfect shot in dynamic underwater environments.

9. Patience and observation: Take your time to observe the underwater environment and anticipate the behavior of marine life. Patience is key in capturing those special moments and behaviors that make your images stand out.

Remember, practice and experimentation are crucial in mastering underwater photography. Each underwater environment and subject presents unique challenges, so be prepared to adapt and adjust your camera settings accordingly.

Tips for protecting gear and ensuring safety underwater

Protecting your gear and ensuring safety are essential aspects of underwater photography. Here are some tips to help you in this regard:

1. Use a sturdy and reliable underwater housing: Invest in a high-quality underwater housing specifically designed for your camera model. Ensure that it is properly sealed and rated for the depths you plan to dive.

2. Perform regular maintenance on your gear: Rinse your housing and camera with freshwater after each dive to remove salt and debris. Follow the manufacturer's guidelines for cleaning and lubricating O-rings or other seals to prevent leaks.

3. Use lens protection: Install a lens port cover or shade on your underwater housing to protect the lens from scratches and damage.

4. Secure your gear with lanyards: Attach lanyards or tethers to your camera and important accessories, such as strobes or lights, to prevent accidental loss or damage underwater.

5. Be mindful of depth and pressure limits: Understand the depth rating of your housing and adhere to it. Avoid exceeding the limits specified by the manufacturer to prevent damage to your gear and potential safety risks.

6. Handle your gear with care: Avoid dropping or banging your camera or housing against rocks or other hard surfaces. Exercise caution when changing lenses

or accessing camera controls underwater to prevent accidental flooding or damage.

7. Be aware of buoyancy: Use buoyancy control devices, such as buoyancy arms or floats, to achieve neutral buoyancy and reduce strain on your arms and back while diving. This also helps prevent accidental damage to the environment or marine life.

8. Practice good buoyancy control: Mastering buoyancy control is crucial for underwater photography. It allows you to position yourself and your gear properly without damaging the fragile marine ecosystem.

9. Dive with a buddy: Always dive with a buddy who can assist you in case of any emergencies or equipment issues. Maintain clear communication and establish hand signals for important messages.

10. Be familiar with dive protocols and safety procedures: Obtain proper training and certification in scuba diving. Follow established diving protocols, such as diving within your limits, monitoring air supply, and performing safety stops when necessary.

11. Respect the environment: Be mindful of the marine environment and its inhabitants. Avoid touching or disturbing marine life, and never remove or damage coral or other underwater structures.

Remember, safety should always be a priority when engaging in underwater photography. By taking proper precautions, respecting the marine environment, and being prepared, you can enjoy your underwater photography adventures while protecting yourself and your gear.

Coral reefs and their vibrant ecosystems

Coral reefs are among the most diverse and productive ecosystems on Earth. They are formed by colonies of tiny animals called coral polyps that secrete a hard calcium carbonate skeleton, which over time builds up to create the intricate structures we see underwater. Coral reefs are found in warm, shallow waters, primarily in tropical and subtropical regions.

Here are some key aspects of coral reefs and their vibrant ecosystems:

1. Biodiversity: Coral reefs are home to an incredible array of marine life. They support a vast diversity of species, including fish, invertebrates, crustaceans, mollusks, and many others. Coral reefs are often referred to as the "rainforests of the sea" due to the abundance of life they sustain.

2. Mutualistic relationships: Coral polyps have a symbiotic relationship with photosynthetic algae called zooxanthellae. The coral provides the algae with a protected environment and necessary nutrients, while the algae provide the coral with energy through photosynthesis. This mutualism is essential for the growth and survival of coral reefs.

3. Importance to marine ecosystems: Coral reefs provide critical habitats for numerous species. They serve as breeding grounds, nurseries, and feeding areas for a wide range of marine organisms. Many fish species rely on coral reefs for shelter and food, while other organisms use the reefs as a substrate for attachment and protection.

4. Protection against coastal erosion: Coral reefs act as natural barriers that help protect coastlines from erosion and reduce the impact of waves and storms. They absorb and dissipate wave energy, preventing direct erosion of the shorelines and minimizing damage from storm surges.

5. Threats to coral reefs: Unfortunately, coral reefs face numerous threats, including climate change, ocean acidification, pollution, overfishing, and destructive fishing practices. These factors can lead to coral bleaching, where corals expel their symbiotic algae due to stress, resulting in their death and the subsequent degradation of the reef ecosystem.

6. Conservation efforts: Conservation initiatives are crucial for the protection and restoration of coral reefs. Efforts include establishing marine protected areas, implementing sustainable fishing practices, reducing pollution and runoff, promoting responsible tourism, and raising awareness about the importance of coral reef ecosystems.

It's important to appreciate and protect coral reefs for their ecological significance and beauty. By supporting conservation efforts and practicing responsible tourism and diving, we can contribute to the preservation of these vibrant ecosystems for future generations to enjoy.

Marine wildlife encounters and capturing their natural behavior

Encountering marine wildlife in their natural habitat is a truly awe-inspiring experience. It allows us to witness their beauty, grace, and natural behavior. Here are some tips for capturing those special moments:

1. Research and preparation: Before embarking on an underwater photography expedition, familiarize yourself with the marine wildlife species you may encounter. Learn about their behavior, habitats, and any specific guidelines for photographing them. This will help you anticipate their movements and increase your chances of capturing unique shots.

2. Respect and observe from a distance: When encountering marine wildlife, it's important to maintain a respectful distance and avoid disturbing their natural behavior. Use a zoom lens or underwater housing with a suitable focal length to capture close-up shots without intruding on their space.

3. Patience and observation: Spend time observing the behavior of marine animals before attempting to photograph them. Watch for patterns, interactions, and interesting moments that can be captured. Patience is key in waiting for the perfect shot.

4. Be mindful of your impact: When photographing marine wildlife, prioritize their well-being and the conservation of their habitat. Avoid touching, chasing, or disturbing the animals, as this can cause stress

or harm. Respect any local regulations or guidelines regarding wildlife interactions.

5. Use natural light and appropriate settings: Underwater photography often relies on natural light. Position yourself to capture the best lighting conditions, such as during golden hours when the sunlight is softer and creates a warm glow. Adjust your camera settings accordingly, such as adjusting the aperture, ISO, and shutter speed to optimize exposure.

6. Focus on the eyes and behavior: The eyes are often the focal point of an animal's expression and can bring life to your photographs. Aim to capture the eye contact and the unique behavior of the animal, whether it's feeding, swimming, or interacting with others.

7. Composition and storytelling: Pay attention to the composition of your shots. Use the rule of thirds, leading lines, and interesting angles to create visually compelling images. Seek opportunities to tell a story through your photographs, capturing the interaction between different species or showcasing the unique behaviors of a particular animal.

8. Capture motion and behavior: Utilize the burst or continuous shooting mode to capture fast-moving subjects or behaviors that happen in a split second. Experiment with different shutter speeds to convey motion, such as freezing the action or creating motion blur.

9. Practice ethical photography: As a responsible underwater photographer, always prioritize the well-being of the marine wildlife and their environment. Do not disturb or manipulate the animals for the sake of a photograph. Be mindful of your buoyancy and avoid damaging or touching delicate coral reefs or other marine life.

Remember, the primary goal should be to observe and appreciate marine wildlife in their natural environment. By capturing their behavior through photography, we can raise awareness about the importance of conservation and inspire others to protect these remarkable creatures and their habitats.

Underwater caves, shipwrecks, and other intriguing environments

Underwater caves, shipwrecks, and other intriguing environments offer unique opportunities for exploration and photography. Here are some tips for capturing the beauty and mystery of these underwater settings:

1. Safety first: Before venturing into underwater caves or exploring shipwrecks, ensure that you have the necessary diving certifications, training, and experience. These environments can be challenging and potentially hazardous, so prioritize your safety and the safety of your diving team.

2. Plan your dive and research the location: Understand the layout of the underwater cave or shipwreck you plan to explore. Familiarize yourself with potential hazards, such as tight passages, strong currents, or unstable structures. Research the history and significance of shipwrecks to enhance your understanding and storytelling in your photographs.

3. Use appropriate lighting techniques: Lighting plays a crucial role in capturing the unique atmosphere of underwater caves and shipwrecks. Consider using strobes or underwater lights to illuminate the scene and bring out the details. Experiment with different angles and positions to create dramatic lighting effects and highlight interesting features.

4. Utilize wide-angle lenses: Wide-angle lenses are ideal for capturing the vastness and grandeur of underwater

cave systems and the scale of shipwrecks. They allow you to capture more of the scene and create a sense of depth in your photographs. Experiment with different compositions and perspectives to create visually stunning images.

5. Incorporate divers for scale and perspective: Including divers in your photographs can provide a sense of scale and perspective, showcasing the size and grandeur of the underwater cave or shipwreck. Position divers strategically to add visual interest and depth to your compositions.

6. Pay attention to details: Underwater caves and shipwrecks often have intricate details, such as rock formations, coral growth, or remnants of the ship's structure. Take the time to explore and capture these details, as they can add depth and texture to your photographs.

7. Tell a story: Use your photographs to tell a story about the underwater cave or shipwreck. Capture the sense of exploration, the history behind the shipwreck, or the mystery of the underwater cave. Look for unique angles, interesting compositions, and captivating moments that convey the atmosphere and emotions of the environment.

8. Experiment with long exposures: In low-light environments like underwater caves, long exposures can create stunning effects. Try using a tripod or stabilizing your camera on a stable surface to capture long exposures that show the movement of water or the play of light in the cave.

9. Post-processing: Once you have captured your images, post-processing can enhance the mood and atmosphere of your underwater cave or shipwreck photographs. Adjust the contrast, saturation, and white balance to bring out the details and colors. Experiment with black and white conversions to emphasize the textures and

shapes.

Remember to always prioritize safety and conservation when exploring these unique underwater environments. Respect any guidelines or restrictions in place to protect the delicate ecosystems and historic sites. Through your photography, you can share the wonder and beauty of these captivating underwater worlds with others and inspire them to appreciate and protect these remarkable environments.

Conveying narratives through underwater images

Conveying narratives through underwater images is a powerful way to tell stories and evoke emotions. Here are some tips to help you create compelling narratives with your underwater photography:

1. Choose a subject: Determine the central focus of your narrative. It could be a specific marine species, a behavior, or a particular underwater scene. Select a subject that has a story to tell or evokes a specific emotion.

2. Composition: Use composition techniques to guide the viewer's eye and convey your narrative. Consider the rule of thirds, leading lines, and framing to create a sense of balance and draw attention to your subject. Experiment with different angles and perspectives to capture unique viewpoints that enhance the narrative.

3. Context and environment: Include elements in the frame that provide context and convey the environment where your subject resides. This could include coral reefs, underwater plants, or other marine life that adds depth and richness to the narrative. Showcasing the subject within its natural habitat can help tell a more complete story.

4. Timing and anticipation: Anticipate the behavior or action you want to capture and be patient. Understanding the subject's behavior and movements can help you anticipate the right moment to press

the shutter button. Timing is crucial in underwater photography, especially when trying to capture specific interactions or dramatic moments.

5. Storytelling details: Look for details and elements that can enhance your narrative. It could be capturing the interaction between two animals, the unique color patterns or markings of a species, or the delicate balance of an underwater ecosystem. These details can add depth and richness to your storytelling.

6. Lighting and mood: Use lighting techniques to enhance the mood and atmosphere of your narrative. Experiment with natural light, artificial light sources, or a combination of both to create the desired effect. Play with shadows, highlights, and color tones to evoke specific emotions and enhance the storytelling aspect of your images.

7. Series of images: Consider telling your narrative through a series of images rather than a single photograph. Multiple images can provide a more comprehensive and nuanced story, allowing you to capture different moments and perspectives that contribute to the narrative.

8. Post-processing: Use post-processing techniques to fine-tune your images and further enhance the narrative. Adjustments in contrast, color balance, and cropping can help bring out the desired mood and emphasize the storytelling elements.

9. Captions and descriptions: When sharing your underwater images, provide captions or descriptions that provide context and insights into the narrative. Explain the behavior, habitat, or any other relevant information that adds depth to the viewer's understanding of the image.

Remember, narratives in photography are subjective and open to interpretation. Allow viewers to engage with your images and create their own stories based on their experiences and perspectives. Through storytelling in underwater photography, you can inspire curiosity, raise awareness about marine life and conservation, and foster a deeper appreciation for the underwater world.

Environmental issues and the power of visual storytelling

Visual storytelling has a unique power to raise awareness and evoke emotions around environmental issues. By capturing and sharing compelling images, photographers can effectively communicate the urgency and importance of environmental conservation. Here's how visual storytelling can address environmental issues:

1. Creating an emotional connection: Visual images have the ability to elicit strong emotions and create a personal connection with viewers. By capturing the beauty of nature or the devastating impacts of environmental degradation, photographers can evoke empathy, concern, and a sense of urgency in their audience.

2. Raising awareness: Images can be a powerful tool to raise awareness about environmental issues that may otherwise go unnoticed or ignored. By showcasing the beauty of endangered species, the destruction of habitats, or the consequences of pollution, photographers can bring attention to pressing environmental challenges.

3. Promoting conservation: Visual storytelling can inspire action by encouraging viewers to become advocates for the environment. By highlighting success stories of conservation efforts, showcasing sustainable practices, or documenting the positive impact of environmental initiatives, photographers can motivate individuals and

communities to take part in conservation activities.

4. Humanizing environmental issues: Photographs that feature people affected by environmental problems can make these issues more relatable and accessible. By capturing the human element, photographers can show the direct impacts of environmental degradation on individuals, communities, and future generations.

5. Communicating complex concepts: Environmental issues are often complex and multifaceted. Visual storytelling can simplify these concepts and make them more easily understandable to a broader audience. By using visuals to illustrate the causes, consequences, and potential solutions to environmental challenges, photographers can engage viewers and encourage them to learn more.

6. Influencing public opinion and policy: Compelling visual storytelling has the power to shape public opinion and influence policy decisions. Through impactful imagery, photographers can help sway public perception, mobilize public support for environmental causes, and put pressure on decision-makers to prioritize conservation and sustainable practices.

7. Fostering a sense of wonder and connection to nature: By capturing the beauty and diversity of the natural world, photographers can foster a sense of wonder and awe in viewers. This connection to nature can inspire a deeper appreciation for the environment and motivate individuals to take action to protect it.

Visual storytelling has the ability to transcend language barriers and reach diverse audiences, making it a powerful tool in advocating for environmental conservation. By harnessing the emotive power of images, photographers can inspire positive change, drive awareness, and encourage a collective effort to protect and preserve our planet.

Inspiring conservation efforts through photography

Photography can be a powerful tool to inspire and promote conservation efforts. Here are some ways photographers can use their work to drive positive change:

1. Showcase the beauty and wonder of nature: By capturing breathtaking images of pristine landscapes, diverse wildlife, and vibrant ecosystems, photographers can remind people of the intrinsic value of nature. These images can inspire awe and a sense of connection to the natural world, motivating individuals to protect and conserve it.

2. Highlight endangered species and habitats: Photographers can focus their work on documenting endangered species and fragile ecosystems. By showcasing the vulnerability and uniqueness of these species and habitats, photographers can raise awareness about the urgent need for their conservation.

3. Tell conservation success stories: Documenting successful conservation efforts and initiatives can be incredibly inspiring. Photographers can capture the positive impact of conservation projects, such as habitat restoration, wildlife reintroduction, or community-led conservation efforts. These stories can serve as examples of hope and motivate others to get involved.

4. Document the impact of environmental degradation: Photographers can also shed light on the devastating consequences of human activities on the environment.

By capturing images of deforestation, pollution, habitat loss, and climate change impacts, they can raise awareness about the urgent need for action and motivate individuals, communities, and policymakers to make positive changes.

5. Collaborate with conservation organizations: Photographers can partner with conservation organizations to amplify their impact. By working together, they can use photography as a tool to support conservation initiatives, raise funds, and promote awareness campaigns.

6. Engage and educate through storytelling: Photographers can use their images to tell compelling stories about the interconnectedness of ecosystems, the importance of biodiversity, and the role of individuals in conservation. They can accompany their photographs with informative captions, articles, or blog posts to educate and engage viewers in a deeper understanding of the issues at hand.

7. Share images through exhibitions and publications: Photographers can exhibit their work in galleries, museums, and public spaces, or publish their images in books, magazines, and online platforms. These platforms provide opportunities to reach a wider audience and engage them in conversations about conservation.

8. Collaborate with scientists and researchers: By collaborating with scientists and researchers, photographers can contribute to scientific documentation and conservation efforts. Their images can be used in research publications, conservation assessments, and environmental impact assessments, providing visual evidence and support for conservation initiatives.

Through their compelling images and stories, photographers

have the power to evoke emotions, create awareness, and inspire action towards conservation. By sharing the beauty, fragility, and interconnectedness of our natural world, they can ignite a sense of responsibility and empower individuals to make a positive difference in protecting our planet.

Planning and preparing for underwater photography trips

Planning and preparing for underwater photography trips requires careful consideration to ensure a successful and enjoyable experience. Here are some essential steps to follow:

1. Research and choose a suitable destination: Research different underwater photography destinations and choose one that offers a rich marine environment, clear waters, and diverse marine life. Consider factors such as accessibility, safety, and the specific subjects you wish to photograph.

2. Obtain necessary certifications: If you're planning to dive for your underwater photography, ensure you have the necessary certifications. This may include Open Water Diver or Advanced Open Water Diver certifications, depending on the depth and complexity of the dives you plan to undertake.

3. Gather the right equipment: Invest in quality underwater photography equipment, including a waterproof camera housing or an underwater camera specifically designed for photography. Additionally, consider underwater lighting equipment, lenses, and accessories such as strobes or video lights to enhance your images.

4. Learn and practice diving skills: If you're new to diving, enroll in a diving course to develop essential skills and gain confidence underwater. Practice your buoyancy control and underwater navigation to ensure stability

while taking photographs.

5. Plan your dives and photography objectives: Before each dive, plan your photography objectives and the specific subjects or scenes you want to capture. Consider the depth, lighting conditions, and the behavior of the marine life you wish to photograph.

6. Understand the marine environment: Familiarize yourself with the marine life and habitats you'll encounter to better understand their behaviors and interactions. This knowledge will help you anticipate their movements and capture more compelling images.

7. Check weather and sea conditions: Monitor weather conditions and sea forecasts before your trip to ensure safe and optimal diving conditions. Poor weather or rough seas can significantly impact visibility and safety.

8. Pack essential gear and backup equipment: Apart from your underwater photography equipment, pack essential diving gear, including a wetsuit or drysuit, mask, snorkel, fins, and a dive computer. Carry backup equipment and extra batteries for your camera to avoid any disruptions.

9. Practice underwater photography techniques: Familiarize yourself with underwater photography techniques, such as adjusting white balance, using appropriate camera settings, and composing shots underwater. Practice these techniques in a pool or controlled environment before your trip to refine your skills.

10. Ensure safety and dive with a buddy: Always prioritize safety while underwater. Dive with a buddy, communicate effectively, and follow established diving protocols. Be aware of your surroundings, monitor your air supply, and maintain a safe ascent rate.

11. Respect marine life and ecosystems: Practice responsible and ethical underwater photography. Avoid touching or disturbing marine life, be mindful of fragile coral

reefs, and adhere to local regulations and guidelines for marine conservation.

12. Back up and protect your images: Use waterproof memory card cases and backup your images regularly to prevent loss. Carry a microfiber cloth to clean your camera housing and lenses between dives.

By following these steps, you can ensure a well-planned and successful underwater photography trip, allowing you to capture stunning images of the marine world and create lasting memories.

Destination highlights and must-visit underwater photography spots

There are numerous breathtaking underwater photography spots around the world that offer diverse marine environments and captivating subjects. Here are some destination highlights and must-visit spots for underwater photography:

1. Great Barrier Reef, Australia: The Great Barrier Reef is the world's largest coral reef system, offering an abundance of marine life and vibrant coral formations. It is a UNESCO World Heritage Site and a haven for underwater photographers.

2. Maldives: The Maldives is renowned for its crystal-clear waters, colorful coral reefs, and diverse marine species. It offers excellent opportunities to photograph manta rays, whale sharks, reef sharks, and an array of tropical fish.

3. Raja Ampat, Indonesia: Raja Ampat is located in the heart of the Coral Triangle and is known for its exceptional biodiversity. It boasts stunning coral gardens, unique marine species, and impressive underwater landscapes.

4. Galapagos Islands, Ecuador: The Galapagos Islands offer a unique opportunity to photograph iconic species such as sea lions, marine iguanas, and Galapagos penguins. The archipelago is a UNESCO World Heritage Site and a renowned destination for underwater photographers.

5. Palau: Palau is a Micronesian paradise with an abundance of underwater wonders. It is famous for

its vibrant coral reefs, underwater caves, and the mesmerizing Jellyfish Lake, where you can capture incredible images of stingless jellyfish.

6. Komodo National Park, Indonesia: Komodo National Park is home to the famous Komodo dragons, but its underwater world is equally captivating. The park offers stunning coral gardens, dramatic seascapes, and encounters with manta rays, turtles, and various fish species.

7. Socorro Islands, Mexico: The Socorro Islands, also known as the Revillagigedo Archipelago, attract divers and underwater photographers with their encounters with giant Pacific manta rays, humpback whales, and schools of hammerhead sharks.

8. Baja California, Mexico: Baja California is a hotspot for marine life, including sea lions, whale sharks, dolphins, and gray whales. It offers opportunities for underwater photography in unique settings such as kelp forests and mangroves.

9. Red Sea, Egypt: The Red Sea is renowned for its clear waters and vibrant coral reefs. It is home to an array of marine life, including colorful fish, turtles, and various species of sharks. Popular spots include Sharm El Sheikh, Hurghada, and Dahab.

10. Andaman and Nicobar Islands, India: The Andaman and Nicobar Islands offer pristine waters, untouched coral reefs, and a rich marine biodiversity. It is an excellent destination for capturing images of vibrant coral reefs, macro critters, and even dugongs.

These are just a few examples of exceptional underwater photography destinations. Each offers its unique attractions and opportunities to capture the beauty and diversity of the underwater world. Remember to research the specific seasons, marine life migrations, and diving conditions for each destination to plan your visit accordingly.

Editing techniques for enhancing underwater photographs

Editing underwater photographs is an important step in bringing out the best in your images and enhancing the colors, clarity, and overall impact. Here are some editing techniques specific to underwater photography:

1. White Balance Adjustment: Underwater images can have a color cast due to the water's filtering effect. Adjust the white balance to restore accurate colors. Use the white balance dropper tool or manually adjust the color temperature and tint to achieve natural-looking tones.

2. Contrast and Clarity: Enhance the contrast and clarity to bring out the details and make the subjects pop. Use adjustments like curves, levels, or the clarity slider to add depth and definition to the image.

3. Color Correction: Fine-tune the colors to make them vibrant and balanced. Adjust the saturation and vibrance sliders to enhance the colors of the underwater scene. Use targeted adjustments or selective editing to adjust specific colors if needed.

4. Sharpening and Noise Reduction: Underwater images can sometimes be soft or have noise due to water movement or higher ISO settings. Apply selective sharpening techniques to enhance details, and use noise reduction tools to reduce graininess without sacrificing too much detail.

5. Spot Removal and Retouching: Clean up any unwanted

distractions, such as backscatter or debris, using spot removal tools. Retouching tools can also be used to remove minor blemishes or distractions in the frame.

6. Cropping and Composition: Evaluate the composition and consider cropping if necessary to improve the image's visual impact. Experiment with different cropping ratios to create a more balanced and compelling composition.

7. Underwater Specific Filters: Some editing software or plugins offer filters specifically designed for underwater photography. These filters can help to restore lost colors, reduce haze, and enhance underwater details.

Remember, editing is subjective, and it's important to maintain a balance between enhancing the image and maintaining its natural appearance. It's also helpful to reference other underwater photographs or seek feedback from fellow photographers to refine your editing skills and achieve the desired look for your images.

Platforms for showcasing and sharing underwater photography

There are several platforms available for showcasing and sharing your underwater photography with a wider audience. Here are some popular platforms specifically geared towards photographers:

1. Instagram: Instagram is a widely used social media platform for sharing photos. It offers a visually appealing interface and allows you to reach a large audience by using relevant hashtags, engaging with other photographers, and utilizing Instagram Stories and IGTV for more immersive content.

2. Flickr: Flickr is a dedicated photo-sharing platform that allows you to organize your images into albums and join communities of like-minded photographers. It offers features such as tags, comments, and the ability to license your images for commercial use.

3. 500px: 500px is an online photography community that focuses on high-quality images. It provides a platform for photographers to share their work, receive feedback, and participate in contests. It also allows you to sell your images through their marketplace.

4. SmugMug: SmugMug is a platform that enables photographers to create customizable portfolios and online galleries. It offers various display options, allows for e-commerce integration, and provides password-protected galleries for client viewing.

5. Your Own Website or Blog: Creating your own website

or blog gives you complete control over the presentation of your underwater photography. You can showcase your work, share stories behind the images, and even sell prints or offer services directly from your site.

6. Photography Communities and Forums: Joining online photography communities and forums, such as Wetpixel, DivePhotoGuide, or underwater photography groups on Facebook, provides an opportunity to engage with fellow underwater photographers, share your work, and gain insights and feedback from experienced professionals.

Remember to choose platforms that align with your goals, target audience, and preferred level of interaction. Consistently sharing high-quality content, engaging with the community, and actively participating in discussions will help you grow your network and gain recognition for your underwater photography.

Engaging with the underwater photography community

Engaging with the underwater photography community is a great way to connect with fellow photographers, learn from their experiences, and gain exposure for your own work. Here are some ways to engage with the underwater photography community:

1. Join Online Forums and Communities: Participate in online forums and communities dedicated to underwater photography. These platforms provide opportunities to ask questions, share insights, and connect with like-minded photographers. Examples include Wetpixel, DivePhotoGuide, Scubaboard, and underwater photography groups on social media platforms like Facebook.

2. Attend Workshops and Conferences: Look for underwater photography workshops and conferences in your area or online. These events often feature renowned photographers as instructors or speakers and provide opportunities for hands-on learning, portfolio reviews, and networking with fellow photographers.

3. Participate in Photo Contests: Enter underwater photography contests to showcase your work and gain recognition within the community. Many contests offer valuable prizes and the chance to have your photos featured in exhibitions or publications.

4. Collaborate with Other Photographers: Collaborating with other underwater photographers can be a mutually beneficial experience. You can team up for dive trips,

share knowledge and techniques, and even collaborate on joint projects or photo shoots.

5. Attend Dive Expeditions and Dive Clubs: Join dive expeditions or dive clubs that focus on underwater photography. These gatherings allow you to connect with experienced photographers, learn from their expertise, and build relationships within the community.

6. Share Your Work on Social Media: Use social media platforms such as Instagram, Facebook, and Twitter to share your underwater photography. Utilize relevant hashtags, engage with other photographers' work, and interact with followers and commenters to build a community around your images.

7. Contribute to Publications and Websites: Submit your work to underwater photography magazines, online publications, and photography websites. This can help you gain exposure and reach a broader audience while contributing to the community's knowledge base.

Remember, engagement with the community should be genuine and respectful. Show appreciation for others' work, provide constructive feedback when appropriate, and be open to learning from others. By actively participating in the underwater photography community, you can grow as a photographer and establish meaningful connections with fellow enthusiasts.

Technological advancements and their impact on the field

Technological advancements have had a significant impact on underwater photography, opening up new possibilities and improving the overall experience. Here are some key technological advancements and their impact on the field:

1. Underwater Camera Technology: Advances in camera technology have made underwater photography more accessible and versatile. Waterproof and rugged camera options, such as compact point-and-shoot cameras and action cameras, have become popular choices for capturing underwater images. Additionally, mirrorless and DSLR cameras with underwater housing allow for more advanced manual control and interchangeable lenses, providing higher image quality and creative flexibility.

2. Underwater Housing and Accessories: The development of lightweight and durable underwater housings has made it easier to protect cameras in challenging underwater environments. These housings are designed to maintain the camera's functionality while providing a watertight seal. Furthermore, underwater photography accessories such as strobes, underwater lights, and color-correction filters have improved the ability to capture vibrant and well-lit underwater scenes.

3. Advanced Auto-Focus and Metering Systems: Modern cameras feature advanced auto-focus and metering

systems that can track and capture fast-moving subjects underwater. These technologies, such as phase-detection autofocus and matrix metering, help photographers achieve sharper images and accurate exposure in dynamic underwater environments.

4. High-Resolution Image Sensors: The advancement of high-resolution image sensors allows for capturing more detail and producing larger prints without compromising image quality. Higher pixel counts provide greater flexibility for cropping and post-processing while maintaining sharpness and clarity in underwater photographs.

5. Image Stabilization: The introduction of in-camera and lens-based image stabilization systems has been a game-changer for underwater photography. These technologies help reduce camera shake and produce sharper images, particularly when shooting in challenging conditions such as strong currents or while handheld.

6. Underwater Drones: The emergence of underwater drones, also known as remotely operated vehicles (ROVs), has revolutionized underwater photography. These devices can explore and capture images and videos in underwater environments that may be difficult or unsafe for human divers to reach. Underwater drones allow for unique perspectives and access to marine life and underwater landscapes that were previously inaccessible to photographers.

7. Post-Processing Software: Advancements in post-processing software have enhanced the editing capabilities for underwater photographers. Specialized software allows for efficient color correction, adjustment of white balance, and removal of backscatter (floating particles) commonly encountered in underwater photography. These tools help photographers bring out the true colors and details of

their underwater images.

Overall, technological advancements have made underwater photography more accessible, versatile, and capable of capturing stunning underwater scenes. They have empowered photographers to explore and document the underwater world with greater ease, precision, and creative potential.

Trends and emerging styles in underwater photography

Underwater photography is an evolving field that has seen various trends and emerging styles. Here are some notable trends and styles in underwater photography:

1. Wide-Angle Perspectives: Wide-angle underwater photography has been a popular trend, allowing photographers to capture expansive scenes and showcase the beauty of underwater landscapes. This style often involves incorporating elements such as corals, rock formations, or shipwrecks to provide a sense of scale and depth.

2. Creative Lighting Techniques: Photographers are experimenting with creative lighting techniques to add drama and impact to their underwater images. This includes using underwater strobes, continuous lights, and ambient light to create interesting and dynamic lighting effects on subjects and backgrounds.

3. Abstract and Artistic Approaches: Some photographers are exploring abstract and artistic styles in underwater photography. This involves focusing on shapes, textures, and patterns found in marine life, corals, and underwater scenery. By using creative compositions and post-processing techniques, photographers can create visually striking and unique images.

4. Macro and Micro Photography: Macro and micro photography, which involve capturing close-up details of small marine organisms, have gained popularity.

This style allows photographers to reveal the intricate beauty and fascinating details of tiny creatures like nudibranchs, seahorses, and corals.

5. Black and White Underwater Photography: Black and white underwater photography has seen a resurgence in popularity. By removing color, photographers can focus on the contrast, textures, and shapes of underwater subjects, creating impactful and timeless images.

6. Split Shots and Over-Under Photography: Split shots, also known as over-under or half-and-half shots, are images that capture both the underwater and above-water scenes in a single frame. This technique requires careful composition and timing to balance the exposure and create visually captivating images.

7. Environmental and Conservation Themes: With a growing focus on environmental awareness and conservation, underwater photographers are using their work to highlight marine conservation issues. By capturing images that showcase the beauty and fragility of marine ecosystems, photographers aim to raise awareness and promote the preservation of underwater environments.

8. Underwater Fashion and Fine Art: Some photographers are merging the worlds of fashion and fine art with underwater photography. This style involves photographing models underwater, using flowing fabrics, creative poses, and unique styling to create ethereal and visually captivating images.

These trends and emerging styles demonstrate the continuous evolution and creativity within underwater photography. Photographers are pushing the boundaries and finding innovative ways to capture the underwater world, resulting in captivating and thought-provoking images.

The role of underwater photography in conservation and education

Underwater photography plays a significant role in conservation and education by raising awareness, documenting marine life, and promoting environmental stewardship. Here are some key ways in which underwater photography contributes to conservation and education:

1. Inspiring Connection and Empathy: Underwater photographs have the power to evoke emotions and create a sense of connection with the underwater world. By showcasing the beauty and diversity of marine life, these images can inspire people to care about and protect our oceans and the creatures that inhabit them.

2. Documentation of Marine Life: Underwater photographers capture images of marine species, coral reefs, and other underwater habitats, providing valuable documentation of the biodiversity and ecological importance of these environments. These photographs contribute to scientific research, conservation efforts, and educational resources.

3. Highlighting Environmental Issues: Underwater photographers often use their images to shed light on environmental issues such as pollution, habitat destruction, overfishing, and climate change. Through compelling visual storytelling, they can convey the impacts of these issues on marine ecosystems and encourage action to address them.

4. Education and Awareness: Underwater photographs

serve as powerful educational tools, allowing people to learn about marine life, ecosystems, and conservation challenges. These images can be used in schools, museums, exhibits, and online platforms to educate and engage audiences, fostering a deeper understanding and appreciation for the underwater world.

5. Conservation Campaigns and Initiatives: Underwater photographers collaborate with conservation organizations, NGOs, and researchers to support conservation campaigns and initiatives. Their images are used in publications, websites, and social media platforms to raise awareness, fundraise, and advocate for the protection of marine environments.

6. Encouraging Responsible Behavior: Underwater photographers often promote responsible diving and snorkeling practices, including respect for marine life, proper buoyancy control, and responsible interaction with underwater habitats. By showcasing ethical and responsible behavior in their images, they encourage others to follow suit and minimize their impact on the underwater world.

7. Sharing Firsthand Experiences: Underwater photographers often share their firsthand experiences and encounters with marine life through storytelling and personal narratives. By sharing their passion and enthusiasm for the underwater world, they inspire others to explore and appreciate these environments and become advocates for their protection.

Through their compelling imagery and storytelling, underwater photographers play a vital role in bringing attention to the wonders and challenges of the underwater world. Their work contributes to conservation efforts, fosters environmental awareness, and encourages people to become active stewards of our oceans and marine life.

Reflection on the beauty and importance of underwater photography

Underwater photography is a mesmerizing art form that not only captures the beauty of the underwater world but also serves as a powerful tool for conservation and education. It allows us to glimpse into a realm that is otherwise hidden from our daily lives, revealing a world of vibrant colors, intricate patterns, and diverse marine life.

The beauty of underwater photography lies in its ability to transport us to an enchanting realm filled with awe-inspiring scenes. From the vibrant coral reefs to the graceful movements of marine creatures, each image tells a story and invites us to appreciate the incredible diversity and delicacy of our oceans.

Beyond its aesthetic appeal, underwater photography serves a crucial purpose in raising awareness about the importance of marine conservation. Through these captivating images, we are confronted with the fragile nature of our underwater ecosystems, the threats they face, and the urgent need to protect them. By showcasing the wonders of the underwater world, photographers inspire us to become advocates for sustainable practices and to make choices that positively impact our oceans.

Underwater photography also plays a vital role in education, allowing us to learn about the fascinating behavior, habitats, and species that inhabit our seas. Through visual storytelling, it encourages us to explore and understand the interconnectedness of marine ecosystems and the critical role they play in maintaining the health of our planet.

Moreover, underwater photography has the power to evoke emotions and create a sense of empathy. It fosters a deep connection between the viewer and the underwater world, instilling a sense of responsibility and a desire to protect these fragile environments for future generations.

As we marvel at the beauty and importance of underwater photography, we are reminded of the urgency to conserve and protect our oceans. It is a call to action, urging us to cherish and preserve these remarkable ecosystems that contribute to the well-being of our planet. Through the lens of underwater photography, we are encouraged to appreciate the boundless wonders of the underwater world and to work towards a future where its beauty can be enjoyed by generations to come.

Call to action for readers to explore and appreciate the underwater world

I invite you, dear readers, to embark on a captivating journey into the underwater world. Take a moment to immerse yourself in the depths of our oceans and discover the enchanting beauty that lies beneath the surface. Whether you're a seasoned diver, an aspiring underwater photographer, or simply someone with a curiosity for the unknown, there is a whole universe waiting to be explored.

Seek out opportunities to experience the magic of the underwater world firsthand. Dive into crystal-clear waters, explore vibrant coral reefs, and witness the grace of marine creatures in their natural habitat. Let the colors, textures, and movements mesmerize you as you encounter a world unlike any other.

Embrace the art of underwater photography as a means to capture and share the wonders you encounter. Through your lens, you have the power to inspire others, raise awareness about the importance of marine conservation, and convey the fragile beauty of these ecosystems. Share your images, tell your stories, and ignite a passion for the oceans in those around you.

But let us not stop at admiration alone. Let us be catalysts for change. Educate yourself about the challenges facing our oceans, from climate change and pollution to overfishing and habitat destruction. Make conscious choices in your daily life to reduce your environmental impact and support organizations and initiatives dedicated to marine conservation.

Moreover, encourage others to appreciate and respect the

underwater world. Share your experiences, your photographs, and your knowledge. Engage in conversations, host exhibitions, and collaborate with like-minded individuals to amplify the message of conservation and the importance of protecting our oceans.

The underwater world is a fragile and interconnected ecosystem that needs our care and stewardship. Let us be the guardians of this realm, advocates for its preservation, and ambassadors for its beauty. Together, let us explore, appreciate, and protect the precious underwater world that holds so much wonder and mystery.

Final thoughts on the captivating journey of Submerged Visions

As we come to the end of our exploration of Submerged Visions, it is clear that the underwater world is a realm of immense beauty, diversity, and wonder. Through the lens of underwater photography, we have delved into the depths of the oceans, witnessed the vibrant ecosystems, and encountered fascinating marine creatures. We have seen how photography has the power to inspire, educate, and ignite a passion for marine conservation.

From the enchanting coral reefs to the haunting shipwrecks, from the graceful movements of marine life to the intricate details of underwater landscapes, each image captured beneath the waves tells a story and evokes a sense of awe. We have celebrated the achievements of underwater photographers and their contributions to conservation efforts. We have discussed the techniques, challenges, and equipment involved in capturing these captivating images.

But beyond the photographs themselves, Submerged Visions has reminded us of the importance of our oceans and the need to protect them. It has highlighted the delicate balance of marine ecosystems, the environmental challenges they face, and the role we can play in preserving them. Through the beauty of underwater photography, we have been encouraged to take action, raise awareness, and make a positive impact on the future of our oceans.

I hope that this journey has sparked your curiosity and instilled a deep appreciation for the underwater world. May it inspire you to explore, learn, and engage with the oceans in your own way. Whether you become an underwater photographer, a marine biologist, an ocean advocate, or simply a mindful steward of our planet, let the Submerged Visions we have shared guide you towards a deeper connection with the wonders of the underwater realm.

Together, let us embrace the beauty, the mystery, and the importance of the oceans. Let us dive into the depths with respect and admiration, for it is through understanding and appreciation that we can become true custodians of our blue planet. The journey of Submerged Visions may be coming to an end, but the call to protect and cherish our underwater world continues.

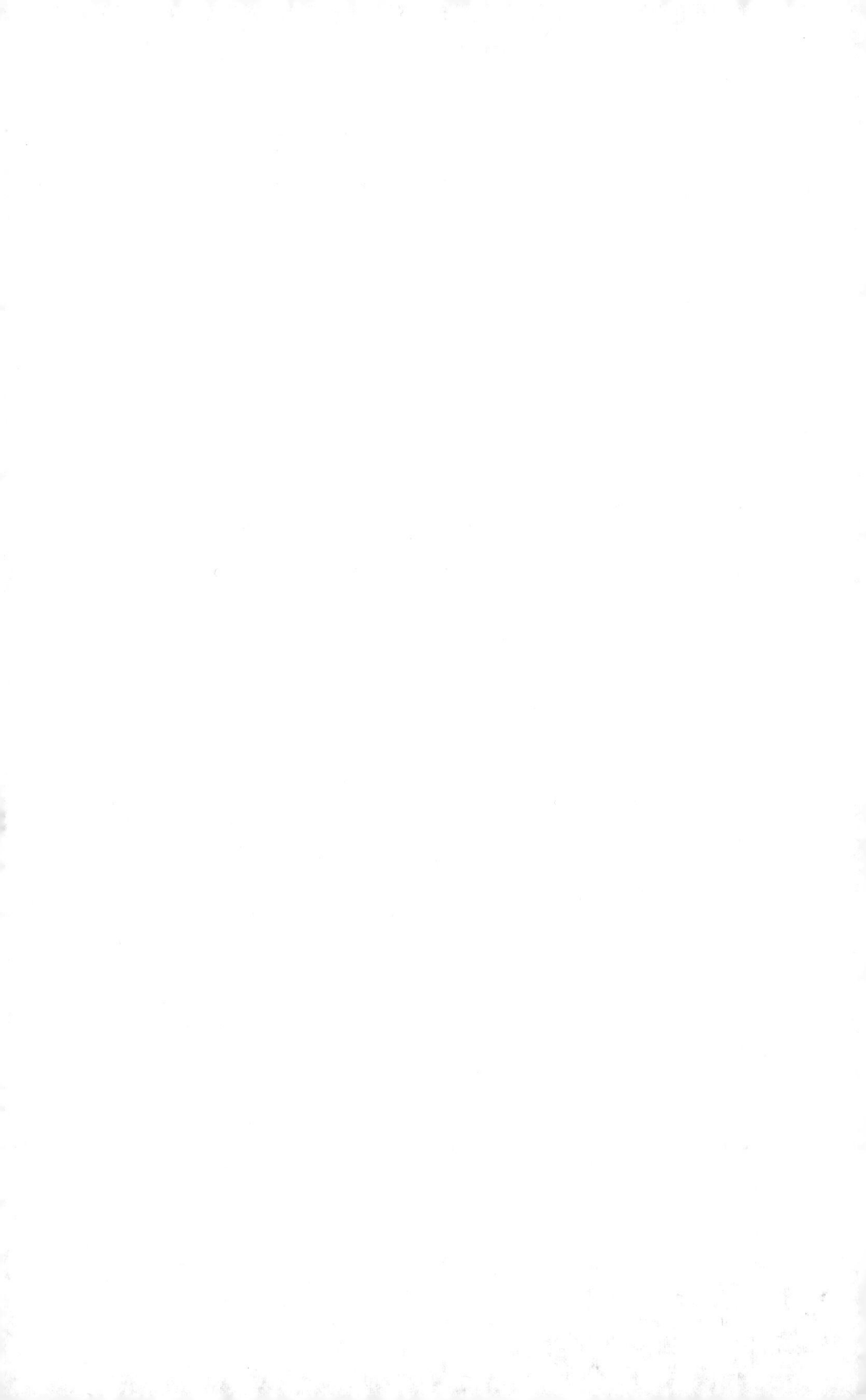